We Need You
Jesus!

Trust in the Lord!

Karen Fitzsimmons

WESTBOW
PRESS®
A DIVISION OF THOMAS NELSON
& ZONDERVAN

WestBow Press books may be ordered through booksellers or by contacting:

WestBow Press
A Division of Thomas Nelson & Zondervan
1663 Liberty Drive
Bloomington, IN 47403
www.westbowpress.com
844-714-3454

ISBN: 978-1-6642-1943-4 (sc)
ISBN: 978-1-6642-1942-7 (e)

Print information available on the last page.

WestBow Press rev. date: 01/12/2021

ROWENA
HOOVER
8-10.8

There is happiness and sadness in the world.
We are looking for hope, love, and peace.

We need you Jesus !

John 3:17 NLT

God sent his Son into the world not to judge the world, but to save the world through him.

John 3:16 NLT

"For God loved the world so much
that he gave his one and only Son, so
that everyone who believes in him will
not perish but have eternal life."

We think toys and stuff will give us the happiness we are looking for, but no we still want more …..

Jesus we need you!

Jeremiah 29:11 NLT

"For I know the plans I have for you," says the Lord. " They are plans for good and not for disaster, to give you a future and hope."

We fill our lives with many things, that we are unable to spend time with God through prayer.

We need you Jesus!

Psalm 46: 10 NLT

"Be still, and know that I am God!
I will be honored by every nation. I will
be honored throughout the world."

We call out to God. Please help me!

We need you Jesus!

Romans 15:13 NLT

I pray that God, the source of hope, will fill you completely with joy and peace because you trust in him. Then you will overflow with confident hope through the power of the Holy Spirit.

The Lord hears your prayers, my dear child?"

"Jesus, thank you for everything!"

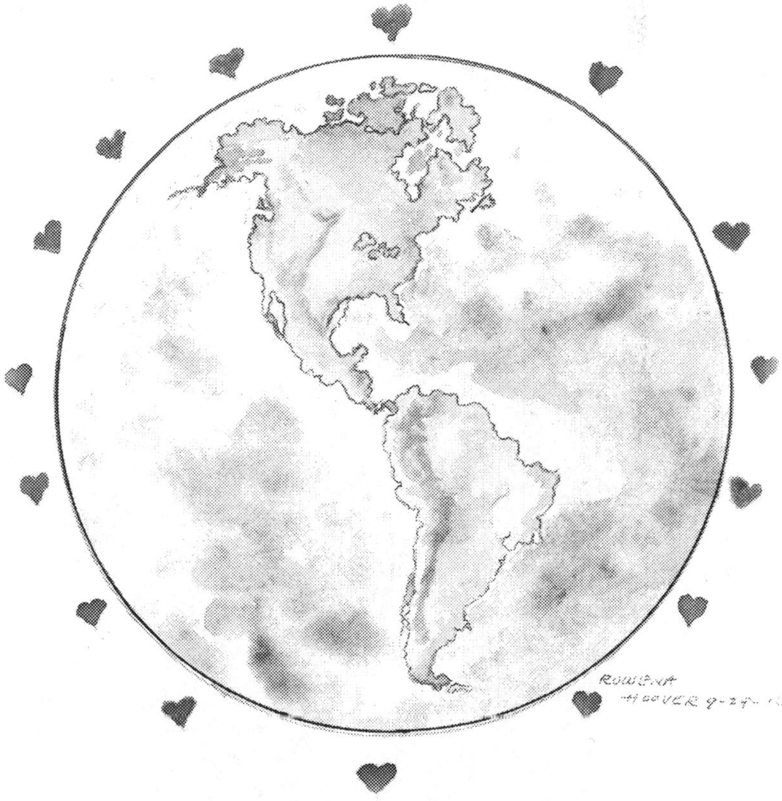
ROWENA
HOOVER

ROWENA
HOOVER
8-25-'20

John 14:6 NLT

Jesus answered,"I am the way, the
truth, and the life. No one can come
to the father except through me.

ROWENA
HOOVER
8-5-20

ROWENA
HOOVER
8-14-20

ROWENA
HOOVER
8-11-10

Praise God in all you do!

We Need You Jesus!

About The Author

Karen Fitzsimmons has written many books, including "Listen My Children", "Perfect Love Cast Out Fear", "Angel Meets Trouble", Joy of Forgiveness", and "Don't Look Back," now " We Need You Jesus".

Karen is a mother of three who knows how important it is to listen and show anyone she comes into contact with that they have value and that God loves them. There is an eternity waiting, so it is important to choose the right path. Whatever your age, God, has a purpose for you. Karen was inspired through her creativity and love for Jesus, to become an author.

About the Illustrator
Rowena Hoover

Born in Mishawaka, Indiana, in 1927, Rowena has followed in the artistic footprints of her maternal grandmother and two uncles. She majored in Art at Asbury College in Wilmore, Kentucky, and attended what was then called Iowa State Teacher's college in Cedar Falls. She was a United Methodist pastor's wife and played piano and organ. She also taught youth Sunday school classes and adult Bible studies in various locations.

Rowena helped raise two daughters and a son. She has taught adult education evening art classes, as well as classes in her own home. She has illustrated a set of First Ladies of America and their gowns,as well as a children's fairy story written by her mother. In addition to Listen My Children, The Secret of Happiness, The Joy of Forgiveness, Will You Be My Friend in English and Spanish, and We Need You Jesus Don't Look Back by Karen Fitzsimmons

Printed in the United States
By Bookmasters